RUNNING COUNTRY ROADS
&
LIFE LESSONS LEARNED

RUNNING COUNTRY ROADS
&
LIFE LESSONS LEARNED

BY RENEE HALVERSON WRIGHT

RUNNING COUNTRY ROADS & LIFE LESSONS LEARNED

Windy City Publishers
2118 Plum Grove Road, #349
Rolling Meadows, IL 60008

www.windycitypublishers.com

Published in the United States of America

ISBN#:
978-1-941478-82-0

Library of Congress Control Number:
2019911075

WINDY CITY PUBLISHERS
CHICAGO

"Treat everyone the same, be honest and fair,
don't be afraid to ask for help and most importantly,
be the best at whatever you choose in life...
I never wanted to be second!"

~ Chuck Halverson

Contents

Preface

CHUCK HALVERSON GREW UP DURING the Depression in Iowa County, Wisconsin, in a rural area between Jonesdale and Waldwick. The population doubled in a single day when his parents, Henry and Clara, along with their 17 children moved to town. Today, Chuck is 94 years old. This is his heroic story, in his own words, about the life lessons he learned from family and friends, WWII, and college football, that all began by running country roads.

Introduction

The Halversons

My father, Henry Gilman Halverson, was born on November 1, 1886. He was the first of seven children born to Ole and Carrie Halverson. My mother, Clara Awila Skews, was born on August 27, 1888. Henry and Clara were married in 1908. My mother died at the age of 65 on June 6, 1954, and my father died at the age of 69 on August 7, 1956. My parents are buried next to each other at Graceland Cemetery near Waldwick, Wisconsin. I still miss them every day.

Graceland Cemetery

My father worked hard on the family farm. He also worked for the Singer Mining Company in their lead mines in Dodgeville. Every day, he would walk 11 miles along the railroad tracks to and from the mines. He worked as a day laborer for a time, too. My father could build or fix anything. I remember riding my white horse, *Thunder*, many miles to fetch his paychecks for him. My father loved to watch me play sports, but he had to work most of the time. He was tough as nails as a man and as a father. He loved all of his children, and I knew he was proud of me.

In addition to giving birth to 17 children, my mother worked very hard cooking and sewing clothes for us and doing whatever was needed to take care of the house. She did a lot of gardening and worked hard with my father on the farm. She had a good sense of humor and taught us right from wrong. My mother loved her children unconditionally with all her heart and always believed in us. I still remember how good her hugs felt and how beautiful her smile was.

She started a tradition when we were all just kids. Once a year, she would have a family reunion picnic. All of our relatives would come from near and far; aunts, uncles, and cousins and that was one heck of a big crowd! Some of us had never even met each other until the day of the get-togethers. Everyone would bring their favorite dish to share. We would eat and eat and eat! We would play softball and meet the new additions to the Halverson family. I have such happy memories of those wonderful times being with my family so long ago.

My mother's family reunion picnic tradition continues to this day at Centennial Park in Dodgeville. Sadly, my sister Alice and I are the only "original" ones left. I still look forward to our family reunions every year.

Clara & Henry ~ Parents

My Beloved Brothers

Henry Clarence

February 24, 1909 - April 29, 1974

Henry was a farmer and then became a Wisconsin Highway Patrolman. He was much older than me and was already grown and out of the house when I was a child. However, we lived together when I was in high school at a farm that he was renting, so we did get to spend some good times together.

Thomas LaVerne

August 10, 1910 - August 14, 1977

We always called this brother, by his middle name, LaVerne. He served in the Army Corps of Engineers at Camp Claiborne, Louisiana, and was a veteran of World War II. LaVerne came to see me compete in sports whenever he could take time away from working the family farm.

Howard Bernell

December 25, 1911 - May 21, 1989

This brother, we also called by his middle name, Bernell. He was a great wrestler and competed on a wrestling team at county fairs. If there was one guy who could lick three, it was my brother Bernell!

Victor LeRoy

August 16, 1913 - November 21, 1983

Vic was a softball pitcher in the Jonesdale leagues. He enjoyed farming, and later worked at Governor Dodge State Park. I remember that even though he was older than me, he would always let me and my friends join him when he went hunting or fishing.

Lawrence Edgar
October 2, 1916 - October 26, 1999

Larry was a softball pitcher for Jonesdale when we were young, and also coached when he got older. He worked the farm with my dad. He started his own company named the Halverson Body Shop. Later, he worked at Klusendorf Motors as an Auto Body Foreman. Larry loved to bowl and was really good at it!

Doral Burdette
March 11, 1917 - November 22, 1990

Doral was a twin to my sister Dora. He did odd jobs and worked the farm with our dad. Later, he worked as a stone and brick layer. Our family nicknamed Doral, "The Judge," because he would always question people. He was very close to my youngest brother Johnny. They grew up hunting and fishing together and they were inseparable. In 1990, I was visiting my daughter Renee for Thanksgiving, walking down the road with my grandson Jason on my shoulders and enjoying the day. Unfortunately, when we got back home, I received a call from my sister, Alice, that dropped me to my knees. She told me that Doral and Johnny had been deer hunting. As Johnny took his stance to shoot a deer, Doral somehow wandered into his line of sight and was killed. I didn't know who to feel worse for...Doral or Johnny, who had accidentally shot his beloved brother. Johnny was never the same after that. This surely was the definition of a family tragedy.

William Everett

October 29, 1918 - October 28, 2012

Bill, who we also sometimes called Willie, helped my dad on the farm. He chopped trees and sold logs to our neighbors. Willie was a great pitcher for the Jonesdale softball team; he could pitch right-handed and left-handed! He always let me hang out with him wherever he went. Willie served in the Battle of the Bulge as a Technician 4th Grade and received the Bronze Star for Meritorious Service in a Combat Zone. While hiding from the enemy, his platoon had to sleep under a bridge on a bed of leaves with only raw potatoes to eat. They ran out of ammunition and were unable to shoot their way out. They were finally rescued two weeks later.

When he came back from the war, he and my brother Wayne opened a lumber business together. He was also an active member of the Blake-Semrad American Legion Post #134.

Harold Keith

January 16, 1920 - October 30, 1995

This brother we also called by his middle name Keith. He worked for Grandpa Skews on his farm and was a big help to him. He was a Staff Sergeant in World War II, serving in Iwo Jima for 4 years. When he came home, he and Larry opened a car repair shop. Keith later owned and operated the most modern gas station in Dodgeville, Keith's Mobil Station. He built a pink house for him and his family next to the station. His daughter Judy still lives there today.

Wayne Eugene

February 18, 1930 - April 6, 2012

Wayne was a farmer. He served in Korea from 1951 until 1953. He also owned a logging company. His fondness for sports and country music led him to write many songs. Wayne was also a poet and his book, "Poems & Thoughts" was published in 1995. I will always remember the trip we took together to Nashville to record some of his great songs. I miss talking with him about his beloved New York Yankees, and our Badgers, Packers, and Brewers. He was a great cook who never seemed to use a recipe.

John Skews

July 21, 1935 - June 23, 1997

Johnny was the baby of the family. He worked on the farm and later for King Lumber. He served in the US Army from 1958 to 1959. When he was discharged, he came back and worked for the Joe King Construction Company as a cement mason.

My Beloved Sisters

Dora Jeanette

March 11, 1917 - March 8, 2001

Dora (Doral's twin) was very talented. She made costumes for all of us kids at Halloween. She also made Christmas ornaments out of anything she could find. She was a great gardener and loved to bake. Dora had a big heart and was one my favorite sisters. She was a proud member of the "Happy Homemaker's Club" and she never baked a cookie that I didn't love!

Ruth Elaine
1921 - 1960

Unfortunately, Ruth suffered epileptic seizures all her life. My mom and dad would have to hold her down and place a spoon in her mouth so she wouldn't bite her tongue. It was very scary for all of us to watch this happen to our sweet sister. We had to send Ruth to a home when she was a teenager because she needed more care than we could give her. We didn't get to see her much after that because the home was far away from the farm. Sadly, she passed away at 39 years old.

Betty Marie
June 19, 1923 - circa 2014

I always called her Betsy and she loved that name. I was very close to her. Like our sister Dora, she was very handy and could design anything. She worked as a waitress at Rohde's Steak House in Madison. Later, she moved to Arizona. We talked on the phone a lot and always kept in touch. God blessed me with my sister Betsy.

Shirley Mae
April 25, 1926- June 17, 1999

I remember that Shirley was always adventurous. She was very spirited and strong willed. She moved out west and sadly we lost touch as it often happens in large families.

Alice Lucille

June 16, 1928 - present

When they were young girls, Alice and Betsy had a saying, "Girls jump ropes and climb trees, so the boys can see what they wanna see." I always thought they were funny. She is now 91 years old and currently resides in Monroe, Wisconsin.

So grateful to have my sister Alice in my life today

Mary Louise

February 21, 1933 - April 19, 2005

Mary was the second baby of the family and my youngest sister. Mary moved to Iowa and we lost touch.

Halverson Family

And So it Began...
September 20, 1924

Waldwick

I was born at home on Saturday, September 20, 1924. Almost all 17 of us were born at home. There were 11 boys and six girls and I was the 12th child born. My earliest memories are from when we lived on our first farm in Waldwick Township, Wisconsin.

When I was about five years old, we had a herd of dairy cows. My older brothers had the job of milking them. As in most dairy barns, just behind the cows, there was a drainage gutter full of the cow's urine and manure. My job was to hold the cows' tails in order to keep them away from the milk pails, and so that they didn't whack my brothers in the face while they were being milked.

I will never forget the time I went to grab a cow's tail and my brother Vic screamed, "Chuck, watch it! That cow kicks." He barely got the words out of his mouth when I was kicked into the gutter and covered in urine and manure. The only thing that was hurt was my pride as my brothers hosed me down.

Around that same time, there was a terrible thunderstorm. Lighting struck our barn and it burned down. All our neighbors came together to help us rebuild. My father wanted to do something nice as a way of saying thank you to everyone, so he held dances in the new barn. He served his special home brewed beer that he kept in the spring to keep it cold. My brother Henry would play the violin and my father played the banjo. Everyone enjoyed those barn dances!

1

During one of our family barn dances, some boys were picking on my brother Vic. All of a sudden, my brothers Keith and Willie yelled, "Hey, there's a big fight up on the hill." My older brothers Bernell, Larry, Laverne, and Vic were fighting with some boys from Mineral Point and Darlington. The boys from nearby towns always seemed to want to pick fights with the Halverson brothers because we had a reputation for being tough and they thought they were tougher.

The music stopped and my family and everyone at the barn dance ran up the hill to see what the commotion was about. We were immediately joined by our close friends, the McNeill family. Whenever there was a fight, the McNeill's and Halverson's were always there for each other. Since I was only 5 years old, my mother kept me back with her. I remember that she was crying, and it broke my heart to see her so upset that someone might get hurt.

The fighting finally ended in the middle of the night. The Halverson brothers lived up to their reputation and scared the dickens out of those boys. They gave up and ran into our corn field to hide. Early the next morning, while my mother was fixing breakfast, she saw the boys sneaking out of the corn field one by one. They had slept there all night because they were afraid to come out and face my brothers again. My father didn't want us to look for fights, but he didn't want us to run away from them either.

Even though life wasn't easy growing up my father found ways for us to have fun. He would cut down tree branches to make skis for my older brothers. The rest of us would watch them ski from the big window. I remember I used to sit on my father's lap. We would all bet pennies on who we thought would make it to the bottom of the hill without falling.

I remember starting grade school at Woodland School, on Highway 30, in the town of Lone Rock, Wisconsin. There were many cold and windy days that my mom wouldn't let me go to school. She said it was too dangerous for me to be walking over two miles in bad weather. I don't remember much more because, when I was about seven years old, we moved to a farm in Jonesdale.

All we had was a horse drawn wagon that we used for grocery shopping, so that's what we used to move. In those days, people moved from farm to farm every March. I remember seeing tons of people and herds of cattle as we were walking the many miles to our next home which was about seven miles past Dodgeville. We all took turns riding in the wagon and walking. It was like a rag-tag parade! People took everything they owned with them. It was a sight to see and I've never forgotten it.

This Was Our Home

We moved to a farmhouse that I was too ashamed to let my friends see. We had no electricity and only a wood burning stove for heat and cooking. There were three bedrooms. The boys shared one room, the girls shared another, and my parents had their

Our rented home at the Jonesdale Farm ~ 1930s

own room. The younger kids slept three to a bed. We had to sleep crosswise so we could fit. We didn't have indoor plumbing and we used an outhouse except in the winter, when we put thunder mugs (which were jugs for us to use as a toilet) under the beds. We washed up in a large tub with water that was heated on the wood stove. My mother also used that same tub to wash clothes.

The house was always cold so we loved it when our mother cooked us breakfast, because the stove would keep us warm. She used to make the best pancakes and oatmeal, and we all took turns washing the dishes. We had to sit on benches because there weren't enough chairs for everyone. When the chairs got too old, we would chop them up and use them for kindling. We all helped put plastic on the windows to keep the chill out. My sisters Alice and Betsy were also creative. They would decorate our walls with "wallpaper" made from old newspapers. The girls even made homemade paste to keep the wallpaper up.

During our childhood, we all worked like dogs, walking behind one-horse plows and cultivators eight to ten hours a day to tend the crops. We grew corn and oats in order to feed the cattle, pigs, and chickens. We also had huge gardens where we grew potatoes, tomatoes, and all kinds of vegetables that were needed to feed 17 kids and my parents. We lived off the land. The only things we did buy were 50 lb. sacks of sugar and flour so my mom could make breads, pies, cakes, and cookies.

My mother also canned fruits and vegetables, which were stored in large cellars until we went to town to sell them to the general store. What we didn't sell, we ate during the winter. Mom would skim off the cream from the milk we got from the cows to make ice cream. I would help my mother turn the handle to churn the cream. We would take the remaining milk to the cheese factory in town by horse drawn wagon.

Even our holiday decorations came from the land. We would go into the woods and always cut down our own tree for Christmas.

We could not afford to buy any store bought decorations, so my sisters would save up the used tin foil from cigarette wrappers to make stars for our tree. They also cut up newspaper to make streamers for the tree, and then we would color the streamers. In our eyes, those simple holiday decorations were wonderful and made our holiday bright. I've had many Christmas trees in my life since those simple ones, but for some reason those humble trees from times past hold a special place in my heart and I always think of them at Christmas time.

Our dear neighbors, Blanche, Jesse and Art James always helped my family during the holidays with extra gifts for us kids. One year was particularly special. The James family gave us a sled! We had never received a "big" gift at Christmas. We were accustomed to smaller homemade gifts from my parents such as tiny dolls or other small, but special, presents like an orange or some crayons. The whole family was tickled to finally have a sled we could share. Art was like a brother to me and our lives continued to intersect throughout the years with work, booster clubs and our love for the Badgers.

White Boots

My Aunt Cora and Uncle Frank ran a boarding house in Chicago. Every so often, guests would leave their clothes behind. When that happened, Aunt Cora would ship them to us because she knew we had no money to buy clothes. We would be so excited when the boxes would arrive, because for us those were new clothes!

Aunt Cora & Uncle Frank

I remember the time my Aunt Cora sent me a pair of white boots. I was embarrassed to wear them because they were white and they were too big for me. I never liked hand me down shoes because they just never fit me right. I would put the boots away in a closet and go barefoot instead. This worked out fine until there was frost on the ground. It was my job to get the cows out of the pasture and back into the barn. My feet were freezing. I couldn't wait for the cows to have a bowel movement so I could put my feet in the cow pies to warm them. After having to stand in cow pies to keep warm a few times, I eventually gave in and wore those embarrassing white boots. I remember the neighbor boys used to tease me and they would call me, "Mr. White Boots." Even now, 94 years later, it still stings from being called Mr. White Boots.

Flour and Sugar

Girls wore skirts and bloomers to school in those days. We were so poor that my mother used old flour and sugar sacks to make bloomers for my sisters. No matter how hard my mother tried to bleach the words, "flour" and "sugar" off the old sacks, they still would show up on the fabric and it caused all kinds of problems and embarrassment for my sisters. When they would crawl up the slides during recess, the

The Quality Bakery opened in 1928. Today, Brian Crubaugh is the third generation of his family to own and operate the bakery in Dodgeville, Wisconsin.

boys behind them could see their underwear. There was a boy in school named Mickey, who was about my age and he would tease my sisters by yelling at them, "Hey, flour and sugar," almost every day. My sisters would come home crying and did not want to go back to school anymore. One day my father said, "We can't let this go on with the boys hurting your sister's feelings and you need to take care of this," and so I did!

Mickey and his friend Joe used to pass by our farmhouse on their way to school and my father sent me out to take care of things. As I walked over to set Mickey straight about how he was treating my sisters, he started to wise off to me and a fight broke out. He told his friend Joe, "Hold my books until I take care of this guy!" We started fighting and it must have taken at least five minutes until I finally knocked him to the ground. After that, my sisters had no trouble with him or anyone else because the word was out to never cause trouble with any of the Halverson family.

Back Row: Willie Halverson, Chuck Ley, Keith Halverson, Art James, Dick Ley; Second Row: Chuck Halverson, Betty Halverson, Lois Whitford, John Allen Burns; Front: Shirley Halverson.

The majority of my classmates were my siblings ~ Jonesdale Country School

Empty Pockets

I always dreamed of having my own bicycle. One day, our neighbors, the Lye brothers, told me they saw an ad in *The Weekly Mineral Point* newspaper that there was a bike for sale for six dollars. I had been working on a friend's farm for a while and had saved some of my money. I was excited because I finally had enough money. The Lye brothers drove me in their truck to pick up the bike. When I told my mother I was going to town, she gave me an extra dollar to buy a sack of flour.

Our first stop was to buy the bike. I gave the boy my six dollars and asked him to count it. We put the new bike in the back of the truck and then went to get the flour for my mother. When I went to pay for the flour, my pocket was empty. In my excitement, I had mistakenly given the extra dollar to the boy who sold me the bike.

I was very sad when I realized I couldn't buy the flour for my mother and cried when I got home. I told her that I gave the boy too much money. She wasn't angry at me because I was honest with her about what had happened and she saw how upset I was. To this day, I can still remember how disappointed I was in myself for letting her down.

2 My Chance

No Place to Stay

Except for my brother Wayne, who wanted to be a writer and went to high school, my brothers and sisters chose to stay on the farm instead of going to school. They loved the country life. Each of them became successful in their own right, but I knew I wanted something different.

I dreamed of ways that I could go to high school and maybe even to college so I could have a chance for a better future. My biggest dream was to play for the University of Wisconsin Badgers someday.

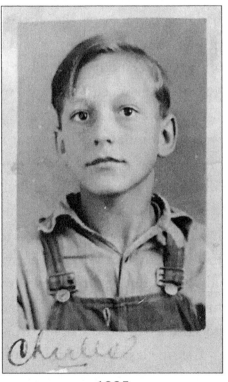

1935

I knew the only way that was going to happen, was for me to be able to prove that I was not only good enough to compete in high school, but to excel. I loved sports. I lived for sports! I believed sports were my only way to achieve my goals.

9

My chance came when my brother Bernell's friend, Elmer Flora, offered to let me stay and work on his farm. It was much closer to Dodgeville High School than our farm. So, when I had just turned 15 years old, I told my loving mother that I wanted to leave home to go to school so I could get ahead in life. I told her that someday, maybe I could even earn enough money to buy them a nice place to live. My mother always supported my dreams and we were always very close. She knew that I could go far in life if I only had the chance…and she agreed with me that this was my chance.

She went to my father and explained, "Chuck wants to get ahead in life and if that's what he wants, then we have to let him go." She convinced him, and on a Sunday in September of 1939, I left home carrying a small bag with my few belongings and walked 11 miles to Elmer's farm to start my new life.

There was a lot of work to be done on Elmer's farm. He had 58 cows that had to be milked by hand. I agreed to help milk the cows for room and board, not for money. Elmer would wake me up at 3:00 AM to start milking and he would go back to bed until 6:00 AM. Then he would join me in the barn. I usually had about 35 to 40 cows to milk before he got there to help me finish. When that was done, I would run 2 miles to school because I had no transportation.

Before classes started, I would wash the blackboards for three dollars a month to pay for my books. That's all the money I had to spend. After school, I was involved in sports, so I couldn't get home in time to milk the cows for Elmer. I was unable to do the job that Elmer wanted me to do, so I had to move on.

With no place to stay, I got myself a room at Hotel Higbee in Dodgeville. I needed money for room and board so I worked some odd jobs around town. One of my jobs was working at a bowling alley wiping down pins and polishing the alley floors. In return, I got a discount rate at the hotel.

The Hotel Higbee was one of the most popular lodging places in Wisconsin and remains a landmark to this day.

I stayed at the Hotel Higbee until I moved in with my brother Vic. He was working and living at the Berg Farm, which was five miles from Dodgeville High School. A neighbor's daughter, Phyllis, used to drive to school and would give rides to other kids for a fee. She would see me running to school and stop to give me a ride. Unfortunately, that didn't last long because some of the parents complained. Phyllis felt bad about it, but she had no choice. I can still hear her voice telling me that she was sorry that she couldn't pick me up anymore. So once again, I was running along country roads.

A year later, Vic moved to another farm in Spring Green. Moving from farm-to-farm was pretty common in those days. I spent the summer there with him, but now it was fall. Spring Green was 18 miles away from Dodgeville and I had to find another place to stay so I could continue going to high school. I didn't know what to do, so I went to my agriculture teacher, Mr. Ken Fox, and told him my problem. I was lucky that he was there to help me. He was like a father to me. He knew my situation and he understood. When I was out of a job and needed a place to stay, he was always there to help me so I could stay in school and play sports.

Mr. Fox

Mr. Fox spoke to his friend, Roy Rule. Roy and his wife lived on a farm seven miles west of Dodgeville. They agreed to let me stay there and I would do chores for room and board. I helped milk the cows, spread hay around in the barn, cut the grass and pulled thistles. If it was raining, Mr. Rule would find me something else to do, like looking for straight nails in the barn so we could use them again. There was *always* something else for me to do.

Mr. Kenneth Fox

The best part of living with the Rules was…they had a car! I would ride to school every day with two of their four sons, Elmer and Norman. I remember making up songs and singing on the way to school. One of my favorite songs was, "The Butcher, The Baker, The Candlestick Maker…they all sing Elmer's tune." I remember that I really enjoyed my time with the Rule family. They opened their home and hearts to me and even came to see me play high school sports.

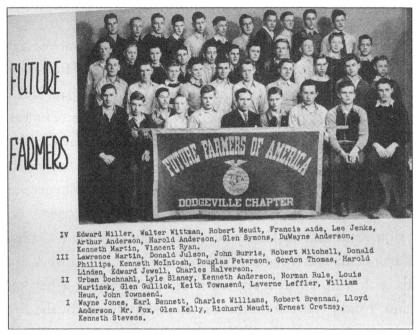

IV Edward Miller, Walter Wittman, Robert Meudt, Francis Aide, Lee Jenks, Arthur Anderson, Harold Anderson, Glen Symons, DuWayne Anderson, Kenneth Martin, Vincent Ryan.
III Lawrence Martin, Donald Julson, John Burris, Robert Mitchell, Donald Phillips, Kenneth McIntosh, Douglas Peterson, Gordon Thomas, Harold Linden, Edward Jewell, Charles Halverson.
II Urban Dochnahl, Lyle Slaney, Kenneth Anderson, Norman Rule, Louis Martinek, Glen Gullick, Keith Townsend, Laverne Leffler, William Heun, John Townsend.
I Wayne Jones, Earl Bennett, Charles Williams, Robert Brennan, Lloyd Anderson, Mr. Fox, Glen Kelly, Richard Meudt, Ernest Cretney, Kenneth Stevens.

Dodgeville Chapter of FFA

Mr. Ted Prideaux

Mr. Ted Prideaux

Another high school teacher who helped me further my education and be a better person was Mr. Ted Prideaux. He was my chemistry and physics teacher. On the first day of class, he asked us to memorize a quote from James Truslow Adams, that I still remember to this day, "There is so much good in the worst of us, and so much bad in the best of us, that it ill behooves any of us to find fault with the rest of us." *I tried to live by these words my entire life.*

Henry's Farm

Sometime during my junior year of high school, I moved again, this time to my brother Henry's farm about two miles from school. It was nice to be able to get to know him and his wife and kids. He was much older than me growing up, so this time together meant a lot to me. I remember he would go into town and play cards with the guys at the Grand Tavern while I was doing the farm work! I laugh when I think about it. He would use any excuse to get out of spreading hay. I'm thankful for the time we spent together.

Oscar Rude and his family lived across the way. He had a beautiful blonde daughter named Marilyn and she used to work in the fields with him. I had a big crush on her! I never let her know, because I didn't have time for a relationship. Recently, she found out that we have the same financial advisor, Steve Gant. She asked him to say, "Hello," to me. Can you imagine, after all these years? It was a big surprise to hear about her again. Sadly, Marilyn passed away recently.

Car Trouble

In high school, I knew a girl named Maggie from Mineral Point. She invited me to her school dance and we had a great time. We double dated with Lloyd Anderson and Rosalie Carey. I wanted to get home early because the next day I was running in the state track meet at Camp Randall Stadium in Madison. No one else wanted to leave early, so we stayed.

That night, Lloyd was driving. On the way home it started raining and his car got stuck in the mud near Rosalie's farm. We had to wake her father, Will, to help get us out. Once he got us out of the ditch, we took Maggie home.

We got about halfway home to Dodgeville after we dropped her off, and then we got a flat tire. Back in the day, we had to jack up the car to fix and patch the tire. By the time I finally got back to Henry's farm, it was 5:00 AM. Henry told me, "You might as well stay home, you can't win anything now." I knew I still had to go because I was the only one who had qualified from my school, I would be running the mile race at the State Championships.

Chuck's State Mile Run - in Camp Randall Stadium - First to break 5-minute records were never kept in those days.

Since it was during the Depression and there were no buses to get me there, the rival coach from Mineral Point agreed to drive me along with one of his track members who had qualified in the 440. Even though I hadn't slept that night, I won the state meet! I ran so fast I was a block and a half ahead of all the other runners. I was the first in our state to break the 5-minute mile with a time of 4:44. I remember it was a really hot day and my sister Betsy was there with me when I won. It meant the world to share the celebration with her.

After the meet, when I got back home, my brother Henry came up to me and said, "You didn't win anything did you?" I dropped my head and told him, "No." Three days later he read in the newspaper that I had broken the state record. He came over to me, smiling from ear-to-ear, and said, "You liar!" and patted me on the back.

Dodger Graduate

During my senior year, I was talking with Mr. Fox about going to college. At this time, he was friends with Mr. Vincent E. Kivlin, the Dean at the University of Wisconsin. Mr. Fox encouraged me to write an essay that might help me to get a scholarship. He even drove me to Madison to meet with the Dean Kivlin, even though I was still in high school. Thanks to his encouragement and support, my dream to one day play college football was one step closer to coming a reality! It was 1944, and I was graduating from high school!

The Dodgeville Dodgers Football Team ~ #33

3 Finally a Badger

Babcock House

My childhood dreams finally came true and I was starting my first year of college at UW! Campus life was so different than my life on the farm, and I knew everything was about to change in a big way. I was humbled by my surroundings and hopeful for the chance at a better future. I remember thinking about my mother, who supported me when I told her I wanted to leave home, and about my father, who let me

Chuck Halverson

go when he wanted me to stay and work the farm. I wanted to make them both proud. This was my big chance and I wasn't going to let them down.

I decided to major in agriculture. Mr. Fox got me in to Babcock House, at 432 N. Lake Street in Madison. It was an affordable three-story house where most of the agriculture students lived. I shared my room on the third floor with two other guys. It was fun and I made a lot of new friends. There was a woman who would come in to cook meals for us. We nicknamed her, "Cookie."

Big Shot

I was anxious and excited to be a part of the University of Wisconsin's football team. I was finally a Badger! A few days before I was to report for practice, I went to the Iowa County Fair in Mineral Point. There was a carnival game where you had to swing a mallet and ring the bell. Not many people were strong enough to do it. I took the large mallet and swung it REALLY hard and rang the bell. Then I realized I had hurt both of my shoulders trying to be a big shot. The town doctor looked me over and gave me a couple of handmade slings to wear. A few days later, when I arrived for practice at Camp Randall, I decided to remove both slings, because I did not want the coaches to know that I had been injured. I ran onto the field less than 100 percent physically, but 200 percent mentally.

I got to meet many of the coaches, including the Head Coach, Harry Stuhldreher. He was a three-time All American, and had been a member of the legendary "Four Horsemen" backfield at Notre Dame in the 1920s. It was a big thrill for me to talk with him. I remember that Mr. Fox and my high school coach, Mr. Friday, had come up to Madison to watch me practice and cheer me on. I'll never forget Mr. Friday telling Coach Stuhldreher that I was a great player. I was thrilled and I was humbled.

Another Calling

I hid my pain from the coaches during practice because I was still trying to earn a position on the team. I was afraid they wouldn't let me play football with my injuries and that could end my college career. It was obvious that I was in pain, so the coaches insisted I have an X-ray. It confirmed that both shoulders were separated. My coaches said, "Chuck we believe you have a big future ahead and you need to heal completely." Months went by until I was fully healed, but there would be another calling… World War II.

Upper left corner: Head Football Coach Ivan "Ivy" Williamson and Athletic Director Harry Stuhldgreher and the Wisconsin football staff, Fred Marsh, Paul Shaw, Mike Bruhn, Coach Ivy Williamson, George Lanphear, and Bob Odell.

4 Out to Sea

1944

USS West Virginia

I was still a freshman in 1944, when I left college and volunteered to join the Navy to fight in WWII. I enlisted because, like my older brothers, I felt it was my duty to serve my country. After weeks of basic training at the Great Lakes Naval Station, which was just north of Chicago, I was put on a train to San Francisco. Then I was sent to the South Pacific on a cargo ship, where I transferred to the *USS West Virginia*. When I boarded the *West Virginia*, I held the rank of Fireman First Class.

Also on board the *West Virginia*, was a Lab Technician by the name of Wilford Kepler from Richland Center, Wisconsin. Once we were all on the ship we were asked if anyone had taken chemistry and physics in school. I was about the only one who had; so they put me in the lab to learn from Kepler. I was working with him for only two weeks when suddenly, he got very sick. He was put on another ship and sent back to his home in Wisconsin for treatment. As a result of this, I was left alone with a medical book to learn everything. It was now my job to tend to a crew of 2,000 sailors. I was the one who would have to give them shots and medicine that was ordered by the ship's doctor. However, my fellow sailors called me "Doc." When the flu hit or the crew got really sick, I would mix up a special batch of medicine that contained alcohol. It usually did the trick. Many times, sailors would come to me and claim to be sick just to get a dose of my famous "medicine."

In addition to my duties as a lab technician, I was also in charge of a 20mm gun used to shoot down Japanese Kamikaze planes. We were anchored near Tokyo for many weeks. Our orders to attack the mainland changed daily. We did not understand why at the time, but we all felt that something big was in the air. This was confirmed, and I will never forget the day the battleship, *USS Missouri* came in and anchored right beside us. The date was August 6, 1945. Not long after they anchored, we heard loud air raid sirens. We were on our guns and ready to shoot down the planes that were surrounding us when the atomic bomb was dropped on Hiroshima. It destroyed 90% of the city and killed almost 80,000 people. Three days later, on August 9, 1945, a second atomic bomb was dropped on Nagasaki.

We were still anchored next to the *USS Missouri* on September 2, 1945, when General Douglas MacArthur boarded it for the formal ceremonies of Japan's surrender. Our ship was so close we could almost reach out and touch him. After the surrender, many of the crew, including me, were transferred to the *USS Wilkes-Barre*, where we spent a few weeks detailed along the Japanese coast reclaiming enemy ammunition. This was scary because some of the Japanese on the mainland were not yet aware that the war was over. They shot at us, but thankfully, no one was hurt. When they learned we were not there to do harm, they followed us everywhere we went, offering us almost anything in exchange for our cigarettes, soap, and candy bars.

Chuck and friend
Herb Lemoine
from Barabog
in China after the war.

Yankee Clipper, Joe DiMaggio

A couple of months later, the *USS Wilkes-Barre* returned home to Philadelphia and we were stationed there. The crew was then down to 1,500 sailors. As a part of our demobilization, we were all ordered to have blood tests before being allowed to leave the ship and return to our wives or lady friends. I only had enough lab equipment to do 11 tests a day; so I talked the ship's doctor into letting me draw the blood and then take it to the hospital in Philadelphia to run the tests. This was great for me because many of the baseball teams I liked were playing in the area. I saw the New York Yankees, the Giants, and Boston Red Sox play. At that time, soldiers and sailors could ride trains for free and never had to pay to go to the games. I

Joe DiMaggio

even had a chance to visit with famous players. I got to see and talk to many of my heroes like Bill Dickey, Hank Bauer, Charlie Keller, and the famous Yankee Clipper Joe DiMaggio. Those were great days…the war was over and there would be new roads to run. (Side note: Interestingly, in 1979, when my daughter, Renee, was an NFL cheerleader for the Chicago Bears she worked alongside Joe DiMaggio! Renee had the opportunity to model and do promotional jobs as a Honey Bear. One of her jobs was working with Joe DiMaggio signing autographs at a promotional event. Renee asked Mr. DiMaggio for an autographed picture for me and she told Joe, "My dad saw you play right after World War II when he was a sailor. You were one of his favorite players. Would you sign an autograph for him?" So, 34 years after I saw Joe DiMaggio play, I received a personalized autographed picture from him…it is a treasure!)

Back to the Gridiron

I was happy to be heading back to college when the war was over. There were many long nights on the battleship when I wondered if I would even make it back. So many young men had lost their lives and I knew just how lucky I was to return home and have another chance to prove myself on the gridiron.

Back to the Gridiron

5 Home at Camp Randall

Racehorse

When I got back to school, I was proud to again be a member of the UW Badger team. I played for three years as a tight end. I only weighed around 175 pounds and those linemen were a lot bigger than me...but I was faster! I was so fast that my teammates nicknamed me, "Racehorse."

Speed wins Halverson varsity post

By FRED ANDERSON
(of the Cardinal staff)

Effort and ambition have finally paid off and end Chuck Halverson has at last made a place for himself on the Wisconsin varsity.

Weighing only 175 pounds, Chuck has had more than his share of jolts from burly linemen in his three seasons on the JV's. But the gritty senior from Dodgeville never gave up and now he has achieved his ambition of playing on the Badger varsity.

Speed has always been a great asset to the 23-year old flankman, and is one of the reasons for his extensive use on offense.

He has a liking for the rigors of the defensive end position, but those fleet legs make him more valuable to Coach Ivy Williamson when the Cards are on the attack.

Aptly nicknamed "Racehorse" by his mates, Chuck is noted for his ability to be the first man down the field on kickoffs. Taking full advantage of Chuck's swiftness, Ivy makes sure the lad is in the lineup when the Badgers kickoff.

One of 17 children, Chuck has had plenty of give and take, and it has reflected in his competitive spirit.

At Dodgeville high school, Chuck was an outstanding all-around athlete, playing end on the football team, center on the basketball squad, and doing yeoman work on the track team.

He copped the state Class B mile title in 1944 in the time of 4:44 and came in third in the high jump.

Football, as one would expect, is Chuck's favorite sport, but basketball ranks a close second, and has supplied some of his greatest athletic thrills. One such thrill came when he potted 12 points to lead his team to a 22-21 victory in a district tournament.

1949

A friendly pat of encouragement from Coach Ivy Williamson

In 1949, I was a senior and I played on the varsity team. That year, we missed going to the Rose Bowl by one game and our team was rated ninth in the nation. I also took a job with the Oscar Mayer Company during that season. Oscar Mayer was very helpful to the UW sports department and often gave us jobs. After the football season, I would go to work at around 3:00 PM and work until 11:00 PM. Then I would go back to Babcock Hall to get some sleep before my morning classes. I remember that in our spare time, not that we had much, my roommates and I used to play basketball and softball. Our teams were sponsored by the Congress Bar.

104 North Butler Street

I met my future wife, Shirley Elizabeth Boyd, while I was living on campus. I was 22 years old and she was an 18-year old local girl. We met at a "social" at the local dance hall. She was working at Manchester's Department Store off the Capital Square when we met. Shirley lived with her mother, Florence, in a house two blocks off of Capitol Square. Her father, Robert, had passed away when she was only five years old.

After a two-year courtship, Shirley and I were married on Valentine's Day in 1949. We lived in her mother's three-story boarding house at 104 North Butler street for a short time until I graduated. Shirley never missed a game and enjoyed cheering alongside the other Badger wives.

MADISON, SUNDAY, NOVEMBER 13, 1949

MRS. WILLIAM GABLE, MRS. JOHN SIMCIC, MRS. CHARLES HALVERSON, MRS. ROBERT RADCLIFFE, MRS. PAUL KESSENICH, AND MRS. KENNETH SACHTJEN

Shirley and other Badger wives cheering on the team!

UW College Graduate

I proudly graduated from the University of Wisconsin in 1950 with a bachelor's degree in Agriculture. Not only was I the first person in my family to finish high school, now I was a real college graduate! My family was so proud, especially my mother, who always believed I would go far in life.

After graduating, I was scouted to play for the Green Bay Packers. Back in those days professional football players were not paid very much. It was not like the high salaries' players earn today, Consequently, I turned the offer down in order to make more money.

Cattle Call

Oscar Mayer

After my college days were over, I took a job as a Livestock Buyer for Oscar Mayer. In the early 1950s, they sent me to their plant in Prairie Du Chien, in southwest Wisconsin. I was honored to become one of their Head Buyers. Every Friday, it was my job to teach the new employees and show them the ropes. I taught them the ins and outs of buying cattle. I made handbooks for each session.

Back row second from the left: Standing with my good friends and work colleagues at Oscar Mayer

My wife Shirley and I lived in a hotel until we could find a home. While we were looking, I received a call from the main office. They were transferring me to their Madison plant. I was thrilled to be able to return to my hometown of Dodgeville and commute to Madison. I worked for Oscar Mayer for 19 years and learned as much as they could teach me.

Halverson Livestock

I decided to leave Oscar Mayer and start a livestock business of my own. I named it Halverson Livestock, Inc. and it was successful for over 60 years. I enjoyed being my own boss and worked hard. I did very well and I made more money than this poor farm boy could ever dream possible.

As part of my business, I had to fly across the state to go to auctions and purchase livestock. I can't count how many hours I flew from sale-to-sale…or how much cattle I bought throughout the years. I remember one time flying to the Don Q Inn, just north of Dodgeville, during an ice storm. It was pretty rocky since we were in a four-passenger plane and running out of fuel. We had to circle for a long time to find a place to set down. The pilot finally got us to an unpaved landing strip behind the Inn. It was one of my more memorable and frightful flights to be sure!

My Friend Joe

I had many buyers working for me and I also hired drivers to ship the cattle. One of the drivers was my close friend from Dodgeville, Mark James. His sister, Joan James, married Milwaukee Braves first baseman, Joe Adcock. I remember taking my kids to see him play. Unfortunately, Joe broke his leg on June 23, 1957 during the Braves Championship season. I would pick him up at the airport and drive him back to Dodgeville. Since he couldn't play baseball, he would travel with me to the sale barns. Joe would buy horses at nearby farms and then have them shipped to his ranch in Louisiana. Joe and I remained close friends until he passed away in 1999.

**Joe Adcock, first baseman with the
Milwaukee Braves**

Our Hearts Were Full

Chuck's Wagon Days

In 1951, I joined the Dodge Point Country Club. The club got its name because it was located between Dodgeville and Mineral Point. It's where I first learned how to play golf. In 1953, I sponsored a team and named it, "Chuck's Livestock." Our team played in golf leagues for many years. I loved that golf course. Some of the members and I helped to rebuild some of the holes and helped the owners plant trees. It was a beautiful place and I had a lot of memorable times there.

With my golf buddies at Dodge Point Country Club

A few years after joining, I was named Social Committee Chairman. We organized many fundraising events over the years. One of the most successful was an annual event that we named "Chuck's Wagon Days." It was a lot of fun and the highlight of the golf season. We built a covered wagon that served refreshments. It was pulled across the golf course by a tractor. I remember that I would sometimes ride a mule from hole-to-hole behind the wagon and play tricks on the golfers.

Owner Rosalie Logue, along with her husband Bill, hosted many parties and events at the Dodge Point Country Club. Rose is seen here getting the mule ready for "Chuck's Wagon Days."

I loved being on that golf course and became friends with the owners, Rose and Bill Logue. They hosted many parties and social events. It was the place to be! I remained friends with them for the rest of their lives and I think of them often. Some of my fondest memories are of bringing my wife and children to the club every Christmas to celebrate with all the members.

**Shirley and I dancing up a storm at
Dodge Point Country Club**

Promised Home

When Shirley and I were living in a small house on Dakota Street, there was a little church a few blocks away that was up for sale. I had always wanted to build a home for my parents, and I saw the chance to buy the church and fix it up as a house for them. My close friend Palmer Schroeder helped me. I was so happy and proud that my dream of giving my parents a new home had actually come true. I don't know who teared up more, my folks or me, on the day they moved in.

Sadly, my mother passed away a couple of years later. I'll never forget the call I got from my brother Johnny, that she was having a heart attack. By the time I got there, she had already passed away. I didn't get the chance to say goodbye, but I know in my heart how much she loved me and that she was proud of me.

Soon after mom's death, our son Chuckie was born. I was so happy that my father was there with us at the hospital for the birth of my first child. The next year, our daughter Renee was born. In spite of losing a baby, Heidi Ann, through a tragic miscarriage, our home and our hearts were full.

A few months later, we lost my father after a long illness. I am grateful for the time I had with him and that he got to meet my wife and both of my children. I will never forget the lessons he taught me.

Old Bricks

Shirley and I had been talking about building a new home for our family. We needed a loan, so I went to Strong's Bank. When they asked me how much I would need to borrow, I told them $10,500. The banker replied, "If you can build it for that amount, I'll give you the loan." We knew we could do it. Palmer Schroeder and I did most of the inside work. He was a great handyman and did the electrical and plumbing work. He was a huge help and a great friend to us.

My parents' house was torn down shortly after my father passed away, and I used some of their old bricks to build the new house. The bricks reminded me of the first time my parents saw the home that I had always dreamed of giving them, and this made our new house even more special, a combination of old and new.

Our house was in a newer area of town. There were plenty of kids for Chuckie and Renee to play with, and we made a lot of new friends in the neighborhood. Since we were only the second family in town to own a TV set, the neighbors would stop by to watch TV and socialize with us often.

Muskies

1950 was a year when playing football re-entered my life. I became a member of the Wausau Muskies, a semi-pro football team that was a member of the Central States Professional League. I was working full-time for Oscar Mayer as Head Livestock Buyer at that time. Consequently, finding the spare time to practice with the Muskies proved to be very challenging. I practiced with them as much as I could, but certainly not as much as I wanted to! The result of this meant that I was only really able to play defense, even though I had been primarily an offensive player in the past. However, in spite of my limited practice time I was still able to be a part of this team, and needless to say being back in football was fun for me!

8 There's a New Store in Town

Shirley's Tots & Teen Shop

Shirley loved fashion and had experience in the retail world. So she opened a clothing store called "Shirley's Tots & Teen Shop." Her store was an immediate hit. We were off to a good start together.

We met Ellen Ann and Joe Weiskircher, who owned "Bucky's Inn." It was located right next door to Shirley's store. We all became very close friends. We would talk for hours about everything and anything. We didn't always agree, but we always respected each other's point of view.

Shirley's Tots & Teen Shop
Left to Right: Ann, Sue, and Pat Anderson; Lori, Bev, and Rick
Bilkey; and Shirley Halverson

Shirl-Ann's

In 1960, Ellen Ann and Shirley decided to become partners and open their own store, "Shirl-Ann's." The store carried women's upscale designer clothing. Shirley and Ellen Ann loved going on monthly buying trips to Chicago together. Their new store was very popular. People came from all over town to shop and socialize there. They even held fashion shows and luncheons in neighboring towns. "Shirl-Ann's" was starting to make a real name for itself!

In 1959, Shirley and I thought it might be a good idea to move our home closer to the center of town and build a two-story flat right across the street from Quality Bakery. We were lucky to be so close to the famous and delicious chocolate bismarcks that the Crubaugh family still makes today after 91 years in business. Our family and the store would be in a better location and we would all be in the same building.

Our apartment was on the top floor, "Shirl-Ann's" was on the main level and the basement was later rented out to "The Betty Hayes Dance School." Behind the building, there was a backyard. In the winter, I used to freeze it over and make an ice-skating rink for the kids.

**Fashion Icons of
Dodgeville
Ellen Ann & Shirley**

Oyster Stew

In 1966, we used the land behind the store to build an addition, a beauty shop called "The Golden Touch." There was just enough room to add an apartment for the owner, Donna Tallard, who was also Shirley's good friend. The new store was in a great location at 141 N. Iowa. It was next door to Perkins Grocery and in the center of the business district. There were always people walking by. Good friends as well as local celebrities stopped in to shop there. Shortly after the shop opened, Donna hired Carol Higgins. They were always laughing and it was a fun place to be. Customers from "Shirl-Ann's" would go there to get their hair done after a long day of shopping. It became one of the most popular beauty shops in town.

"Shirl-Ann's" always stayed open late on Christmas Eve in case there were last minute shoppers. When the store finally closed for the night, everyone would come up to our apartment, where I would be cooking my mother's oyster stew and making eggnog to share with them. It became a tradition. Afterward, my family would go to the Schroeder's house for their annual Christmas Eve parties. Mary Lou would make her famous crab dip and homemade chocolate fudge and all the kids would sing Christmas carols around the piano.

Special Customer

Mrs. Frank Lloyd Wright was a frequent customer of Shirl-Ann's. I remember that Mrs. Wright and her dog would arrive in a chauffeured car whenever she would shop at the store. Once inside, she would sit in her favorite chair, and Shirley and Ellen Ann would show her clothing they thought she might like. She always bought something! During the winter months, Mrs. Wright would stay in Scottsdale. When Shirley and Ellen Ann had their sales, Mrs. Wright had her son-in-law fly into Madison just to shop at the store.

Mrs. Wright invited us to many of her dinner parties and we got to meet a lot of interesting people there. A live orchestra always played as dinners were being served. I remember having to rent a tux to wear to those parties. Everything was very fancy. Their home was a country estate. It wasn't my cup of tea, but I did enjoy meeting the architects and touring the grounds. Years later, we would build a Frank Lloyd Wright style home of our own.

9 The Log Cabin

Ludden Lake

In the 1960s, we owned a log cabin on Ludden Lake, which was named in honor of Mineral Point's "local boy" Allen Ludden, best known as the host of *Password* and the husband of comedienne Betty White. The lake was seven miles away from our home in Dodgeville. Almost every weekend in the summer, my family would go there with our friends, the Schroeder family. The cabin was small. It had two bedrooms, a wood burning stove, and only one bathroom. You can imagine what it was like there with 14 people between us! During the day, we all would water ski and swim in the lake. One day, I decided I needed a new project, so I dug a swimming pool for us all. At night, the kids would roast marshmallows and catch fire-flies in jars. At bedtime, all eight kids slept in sleeping bags scattered across the living room. We didn't spend as much time at the cabin in the winter, but when we did, I remember the kids would sled down a hill and have contests to see who could sled the farthest out onto the lake.

My daughter Renee was excited to test out the diving board

The Tall Tree

Many years later in 1977 at our Frank Lloyd Wright style home, I took Chuck and Renee out to the woods with me to cut down a tree. It didn't look very tall while we were cutting it down but when we got it back home and tried to stand it up, it brushed against the 22 ft. high ceiling! We had many beautiful trees, but that's the one none of us will ever forget. It took a long time to decorate and took up the whole room! I had to take a chain saw to it just to get it out of the house. It was such a happy place for my family and friends.

Ludden Lake Golf Course and Country Club

So, in 1977, I decided to buy more land around the cabin. I wanted to build a golf course so I could putt around. Then a lightbulb went off in my head and I got the idea to build homes and a nine-hole golf course around the lake. I thought it would be a great place for a new community and would also be good for businesses in the area.

The Ludden Lake Golf Course and Country Club project was approved by the county and we started building. Besides the nine-hole golf course, we also built a clubhouse. The lower level included a bar area, restrooms, and a changing facility. There was also a pool located next to the building.

New Golf Complex Takes

It all started with the creation of a 78-acre lake approximately 14 years ago, and it has now mushroomed into a nine-hole golf course and complex west of Mineral Point.

Owned and operated by Charles Halverson and Halverson Livestock, Inc., the Ludden Lake Golf Course and Country Club is nearing completion about a mile and a half west of Mineral Point. The complex is located on Lake Road off of CTH "Q" and STH 39.

Halverson and a number of other area people started the Ludden Lake project with the intention of creating home sites to promote business in the area. Several sites were plotted and homes were built on the east side of the lake, and recently, Halverson purchased 60 acres on the west side.

With that land, he first had the idea to build a country cottage. Next to the cabin, he thought he would put in two golf greens in the valley to "putt around on" in his spare time. However, the idea skyrocketed, and a nine-hole course resulted.

The course, when complete, will include one par five 530-yard course, three par threes, and five par fours. The course will be a par 34. One of the holes will be especially challenging, with a boat needed to cross an area approximately 130 yards across Ludden Lake. Three of the nine holes are presently ready for use, and all nine should be in good shape by next spring.

Seven of the holes could be in use by September 1, Halverson says.

To go along with the golf course, a club house has been constructed on the Halverson property. The lower level includes a bar area, and rest room and changing facilities for a 51 x 20 foot pool which is located next to the building. The pool is for member use only, and should be ready for swimming by early next week.

Patio and cookout areas are located outside the clu... and four furnished c... level. The apartments, too nearing completion, and w... ready for occupancy som... next week. The apartment...

Charles Halverson on the balcony of one of the efficiency apartments at the L... apartments overlook the golf course and lake.

Ludden Lake Golf Course and Country Club

10

Life with Chuck Jr. and Renee

Family Vacations

Growing up the way I did, I never even gave a thought to traveling or going on a vacation. The only time I had ever traveled was to football games and to fight in the war. Once I had my kids, I promised myself that they would get to see more of the world than I did. I wanted us to see new places for the first time together as a family and make memories they would never forget.

When the kids were young, Shirley and I surprised them with a trip to Florida. It was the first time the kids had ever been out of Wisconsin and they were very excited. They had never seen the ocean and had the time of their lives looking for seashells, walking in the sand, and playing in the waves. It was a gift I never expected to be able to give to my family and I was thankful. As the years went on, we took many more family vacations. We went to the Bahamas, and back to Florida a few times. Shirley and I just loved Las Vegas and went there often over the years. The last time we were there, we got tickets to see The Supremes play their farewell concert.

Sunday Rituals

Sunday mornings were always special times for us. I would get up early and make pancakes for Shirley and the kids. After breakfast, we would all walk to Dodgeville Methodist Church for Sunday services. Then, we would walk home and watch *Dairyland Jubilee* on TV. *Dairyland Jubilee* was an extravaganza type of show that aired for thirteen straight years on WKOW-TV. The show featured polka bands and people dancing the polka. We also liked to watch the roller derby games that were broadcast. Of course though, during football season we watched every Green Bay Packers game and never missed a one! These were our Sunday rituals for more years than I can remember, and they were very happy times.

In the early 1970s, the more than 100-year old Dodgeville Methodist Church was torn down to make way for a much-needed new church. I purchased one of the stained-glass windows from the old church and I had it built into the ceiling of the dining room of our Frank Lloyd Wright style house. It hung over our dining room table. I added backlighting behind the window and that really brought the window to "life!" Through the years that beautiful window was always a conversation starter.

Trout Fishing

I taught Chuckie and Renee how to swim and fish. We spent many hours trout fishing in creeks and ponds in the area. We planted pumpkins and watermelons together. I wanted to share my love of the land with them. I wanted them to know how it felt to get their hands dirty and how to bait their own hooks. It brought me back to my roots and I wanted them to experience the things I enjoyed when I was a young boy on the farm. We had lots of fun together when Chuckie and Renee were growing up.

11

Badgers, Packers, and...Bears

Badger Booster Club

In 1968, Dodge Point Country Club created and sponsored the "Iowa County Badger Boosters." The purpose of the club was to raise money for the UW Athletic Department which needed help at the time. We had the support of all the Head Coaches from the various departments including my dear friend, Elroy "Crazy Legs" Hirsch. He was a former Badger and pro football Hall of Famer, and the current Athletic Director at UW.

Elroy "Crazy legs" Hirsch and I were great friends. We both loved the Badgers!

In 1978, The Booster Club sold tickets and raffled off chances for Badger fans to meet Elroy and the other coaches. Many years later, my daughter Renee, who was a Chicago Honey Bear, along with four of her teammates, made appearances and performed. I was so proud to have them there. We held golf outings and banquets. These events were very popular and got more successful with each passing year. All the money we raised went to support athletics at UW. None of this would have been possible without the help of Rose and Bill Logue. After they sold Dodge Point, the new owners, Ralph and Tony Pitts continued our tradition, which lasted until 1981.

The Booster Club also sponsored bus trips to away games between the Badgers and our rivals, the Iowa Hawkeyes. For 20 years, friends shuttled back and forth from Dodge Point to Iowa City, depending on where the game was being played. Afterward, we would all get together for dinner and dancing, and to celebrate the winners and console the losers. It was another wonderful tradition that raised money for UW athletics.

This event ended when my very good friend, Ronnie Bowman, died of cancer in the late 1980's. Ronnie and I met when we were in the cattle business together. We were close friends for over 30 years and our families were also close. Ronnie was an avid Hawkeye fan and a member and past president of the National I-Club. I hosted when the Hawkeyes played in Wisconsin and he was the one who hosted when the Badgers travelled to Iowa. No one could ever take his place and he is missed by many. The Booster Club raised over $1 million for the UW Athletic Department. We also donated money to the church and high school. I still continue to donate as I can.

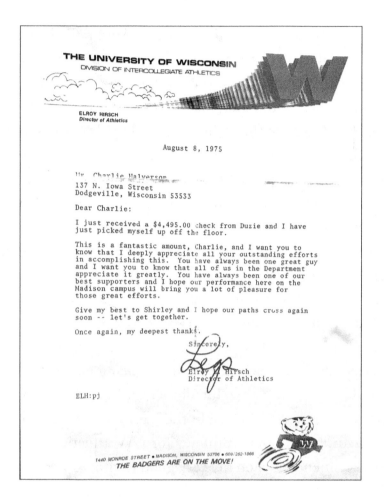

THE UNIVERSITY OF WISCONSIN
DIVISION OF INTERCOLLEGIATE ATHLETICS

ELROY HIRSCH
Director of Athletics

August 8, 1975

Mr Charlie Halverson
137 N. Iowa Street
Dodgeville, Wisconsin 53533

Dear Charlie:

I just received a $4,495.00 check from Duzie and I have
just picked myself up off the floor.

This is a fantastic amount, Charlie, and I want you to
know that I deeply appreciate all your outstanding efforts
in accomplishing this. You have always been one great guy
and I want you to know that all of us in the Department
appreciate it greatly. You have always been one of our
best supporters and I hope our performance here on the
Madison campus will bring you a lot of pleasure for
those great efforts.

Give my best to Shirley and I hope our paths cross again
soon -- let's get together.

Once again, my deepest thanks.

Sincerely,

Elroy H. Hirsch
Director of Athletics

ELH:pj

1440 MONROE STREET • MADISON, WISCONSIN 53706 • 609/262-1866
THE BADGERS ARE ON THE MOVE!

The Terrills

Lowell "Duzie" Terrill and his wife, Alice, were dear friends for many years. Duzie was involved in starting the Iowa County Booster club and a big help with raising funds for the Badgers, schools and local churches for over 40 years. Sadly, he and his lovely wife Alice passed away a few years ago, but I am happy that Duzie's daughters, Marsha, Pam, Patti, and Lori, who he called his four "Mother's Hens," still attend my Birthday Bash at Lot 17.

With my dear friend Duzie...I miss him!

Honey Bear

In 1978, my daughter, Renee, became a member of the Chicago Bears professional cheerleader squad, the Honey Bears. Even

though I was a lifelong Green Bay Packers fan, I bought Bears season tickets so I could watch her cheer. Shirley and I went to every home game and cheered for our daughter. As I watched the games from the stands, football memories from my days as a Badger, always came back. Now, years later, I was watching my beautiful dancing daughter on the sidelines of Soldier Field. The gridiron was in her blood!

Renee Halverson

Die-Hard Fan

My son, Chuck Jr., is developmentally challenged. However, as a son, he is full and complete in so many ways. His sense of humor, kindness, and gentility is never failing. He too loves football, and is a die-hard Badgers and Packers fan, and he got such a kick out of it when his little sister Renee became a Chicago Bears cheerleader. Chuck Jr., takes great pleasure in simple things and reminds me to do so too. I am proud to say that my son has taken himself to his own fullness in life.

I am very grateful for my son Chuck ~ 2019

12 Bittersweet Times

Goodbye to Dodgeville

A sad event that happened in 1978, was that Ellen Ann passed away. Shirley had not only lost her best friend but also her business partner, and it was time to close "Shirl-Ann's." The store would never be the same without Ellen Ann. We rented out our building and started a new chapter in our lives, knowing that we would never forget the chapters that included Ellen Ann. After living in our Frank Lloyd Wright style home full-time we moved to the west side of Madison and Shirley opened another store. She kept the name "Shirl-Ann's" in honor of her dear friend. I continued in the livestock business and we were both happy to be living near our son, Chuck Jr.

Halverson's Frank Lloyd Wright style home

National W Club President

I was President of the UW National W Club from 1980 to 1981. It was an honor for me, a former Badger, to be elected. I was proud to continue the W Club tradition of raising money and providing scholarships for our athletes.

Papa

My daughter Renee got married in 1983. I was so proud to walk her down the aisle. I hired a bus to bring everyone from Dodgeville to Chicago for the wedding so they wouldn't have to drive. I only wish my parents had lived long enough to be there.

With my grandsons Jason and Brian

I became a "Papa" when my grandson Jason was born on January 26, 1987. He was soon followed by his brother Brian on August 27, 1989, the same date as my dear mother who was born August 27, 1888. I was over the moon! Ever since I was a little boy, I was awakened by the rooster's cocka-doodle-dooing and I got pretty good at imitating it. Being able to cocka-doodle-doo was a big hit with my citified grandsons and every time we would get together, they would always ask me to do the rooster call. I loved hearing them laugh each time I did it…even though they had heard it a million times. I love my grandsons unconditionally to this day and I am very proud of them. I enjoy every second that I have with them, and have many fond memories of teaching them how to fish. We also have had many great times tailgating at Badger games through the years.

Saying Goodbye

I lost my wife Shirley on September 18, 2000. She died in our daughter Renee's arms. Her funeral was held two days later, on my birthday. Shirley and I had been married for 51 years. When I look back over those 51 years, I am frankly taken aback by all of the challenges that she and I faced together, but what stands out the most are the triumphs and fun times that we shared. She was a unique woman who loved this football playin' farm boy and I loved her. Shirley is buried in a cemetery right behind where her beloved "Shirl-Ann's" had been.

13 New Beginnings

Meeting Marion

Tailgating with Marion

My longtime dear friends, the Careys, had season tickets at Camp Randall Stadium next to my seats for over 50 years...and once again, football would impact my life in an interesting twist of fate. The Carey's daughter, Jean, played golf with a lady named Marion Falch. Jean brought Marion with her to a Badgers game. Marion and I hit it off right away...a love-match made at Camp Randall! We were married on May 7, 2004. Marion is my favorite cook and we have a good life together. We are very involved with our church, Lutheran Church of the Living Christ, and we have made many fine friends within this congregation. Of course, we have also continued to enjoy cheering on our Badgers and Brewers. Marion has three lovely daughters, Tara, Victoria, and Stephanie, and they have all been very good to us and we appreciate them every day.

"That Cap You're Wearing!"

Sometime in 2005, my daughter, Renee, called to tell me about someone she had met while she was at the dog park walking her Golden Retrievers. She noticed a tall man wearing a UW baseball cap. When she got closer to him, she could see what was written on the cap "Butch & Chuck's Badger Bash."

Renee went up to the man and said, "That cap you're wearing! My dad is Chuck!" The man said, "You're Chuck Halverson's daughter?" Renee told me that she smiled and proudly said, "Yes, he's my dad." The man told her that his name was Cal Vernon and he had a story to share. So, they sat down together on a nearby bench. He told her that he had played football with me at UW, and then said, "I'll never forget what your dad did for me and some of our teammates." He went on to explain to Renee, "The Badgers were playing a game in southern Indiana. We all got off the bus and went to a diner for breakfast. When we walked in and sat down, we were told by the manager that they wouldn't serve the black

Over the course of 30+years, Butch's Bologna Bash drew 10,000 people to the UW Field House. The bash raised more than 3 million for UW athletes and Band. Butch was a dear friend and I miss him. Palmer "Butch" Strickler, UW Athletic Director, Barry Alvarez and me

players. Your dad got up and told him that if he wouldn't serve us, then he wouldn't be serving any of us, and then the whole team got up and walked out." Renee had never heard this story before and couldn't wait to call and tell me she had met Cal in the dog park. When she told me the story, I remembered Cal and what had happened that day. It made me happy to know that she and Cal had a chance to meet.

Go Badgers

When I was 89 years old, I was recognized by the UW Athletic Department and Oscar Mayer, as their Season Ticket Holder of the Game. On November 9, 2013, they honored me for being a season ticket holder for 66 years, and for my fundraising efforts over the past 40 years. I got to be on the field at Camp Randall during halftime and I remember hearing everyone cheer for me…but there was a huge difference between those cheers and the ones I had heard so many years before as a Badger player…this time, my wife, kids, and grandchildren were all there cheering for me too! I never dreamed that my days on the gridiron would sort of come full circle like this. It was one of those stand-out days in life!

Singing the National Anthem next to my dear family friend ~ Rick Bilkey

**Grandsons Brian, Jason and my daughter Renee ~
Camp Randall Stadium**

14 Badger Honor Flight

Off to Washington, D.C.

My daughter arranged for me to be part of an honor flight for veterans to Washington DC on September 12, 2015. When I was told about the event, I was excited and wanted to go, but then I realized that the Badgers would be playing that very same day. I had never, ever missed being at a home game in my life, but this was something very special. I later found out that the Badgers won 58-0 against Miami of Ohio, so it was a win-win day.

Renee was my volunteer throughout the trip. We needed to be at the Dane County Regional Airport by 5:00 AM. She ordered a taxi and it was an interesting ride. We were surprised to find that our driver also happened to be a WWII Veteran! I enjoyed sharing stories with him about our days in the military. When we arrived at the check-in station at the airport, they gave us our badges, jackets and hats. We wore red and the volunteers wore blue. I was very proud and at the same time sad to see that there were only 6 of us there that day representing WWII. I was very  surprised that one of my old war buddies was also on the flight. It had been many years since we'd seen each other. All the veterans had our pictures taken in front of a huge American flag. After that, there was a wonderful Send Off Ceremony as we proceeded through security and boarded the plane. People of all ages, including current soldiers and boy scouts, held up handmade signs and waved flags. They all applauded and shook our hands as we made our way through the line. Even the Badger Band was playing for us as we headed towards the plane. We all felt so special!

We arrived at Reagan National Airport in Washington DC at 10:00 AM. When we stepped off the plane to enter the terminal, there were hundreds of people waiting there to greet us. There were also several buses. Each bus had a tour guide on board. He would use a microphone to point out sights and let us know what would happen at each stop. At one of the stops, I picked up the microphone and started telling jokes. I had everyone laughing and it sure broke the ice! We were all "old friends" by the end of the day.

The first place we visited was Arlington National Cemetery. It was pouring rain but that didn't stop us from getting the full experience. We all got out of the bus and walked over to see the changing of the guard. No one spoke and it was very moving.

Our next stop was at the Iwo Jima Memorial. We took a group photo in front of the statue. We were in awe of the amazing statue of the brave soldiers raising our flag. It was extra special for me to be there because my brother Keith and my friend Fritz Bilkey had fought there. I saluted them and all who had fought so bravely.

Purple Heart

As a Navy Corpsman, Fritz was assigned to a Marine Division that invaded Iwo Jima. Although a rifle was part of his gear, his duties as a medic prevented him from ever using it. When a former Dodgeville classmate showed up, he said to him, "What the hell are you doing here…this place is horrible!" "Get the hell out of here!"

Frederick "Fritz" Bilkey

On March 14th, 1945 Fritz made his way through intense battle grounds, with machine guns and rifles firing everywhere and with complete disregard for his personal safety, to help a wounded marine. While discovering that the marine was already dead, Fritz was seriously wounded by the same sniper who used an illegal bullet.

After returning home, he tried hunting, but the smell of gunpowder gave him flashbacks. Throughout the entire operation on Iwo Jima, Fritz distinguished himself as a Medical Corpsman of the highest caliber, receiving a Commendation Medal For Bravery and a Purple Heart.

We lost Fritz in 1974 while he was delivering mail in the Township of Dodgeville. He passed on at the early age of 50 from a heart attack. He was an excellent athlete and he loved sports. Fritz was a wonderful father to his three children, Barry, Rick and Lori, who I now consider my own and love them dearly. Fritz always called me a "self-made man." I miss him and he will always be remembered as my dear friend and a hero to us all.

Fritz's daughter Lori Bilkey Sanders has been an important part of my life for many years. She is like a second daughter to me.

A Few Surprises

We ate our box lunches on the bus and then headed to the WWII Memorial. The rain finally stopped, and the sun was shining when we arrived. Senator Robert Dole was there in his wheelchair to meet us. He shook our hands and I had a few minutes to speak with him. We talked about baseball and found out that we both were Joe DiMaggio fans. Senator Dole was very friendly and welcoming. It meant a lot to all of us that he was there. Then we were greeted by people dressed in WWII attire. They performed skits, entertained, and even danced with us. We had a great time with them. When we got to the Vietnam Memorial Wall, we were overwhelmed. So many names. So many lives lost.

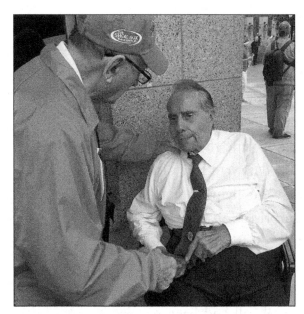

**Senator Dole and I chatting about
baseball ~ WWII Memorial**

**A special moment with greeter
Theresa Werner and daughter
Renee ~ WWII**

Our last stop was the Lincoln Memorial. Coincidently, there was an NFL team, the Miami Dolphins, there at the same time. I started talking to the players and they showed me their Superbowl rings. It was the best way I could've asked for to end the tour. Soon it was time to head back to the airport. The day went by so fast!

While we were flying home, there were a few surprises for all of the Vets. In the middle of the flight, the tour guides cheerfully called out, "Mail call!" Wow, even that brought back memories because mail call had been so very important to us back when we were in the service. Then the tour guides called

Miami Dolphin's player and me admiring each other's football rings ~ Lincoln Memorial

out each of our names, and each of us were handed a large manila envelope. Inside of the envelope were personalized cards and letters that had been written to us by family and friends, thanking us for our service. It was very special and a highlight of the trip. Two of the letters were real stand-outs for me because they were written to me by my two grandsons, Jason and Brian.

Dear Papa,

I've always looked up to you as a role model in my life, the way you have worked and driven hours to support your family, and how you would always visit me as a little kid even though you had hours to drive.

I can't express how appreciative as well as honored I am that you are my grandpa. I've always been touched by your passion for the Wisconsin Badgers, and I relate it to the love I have for my favorite teams. You put so much into everything you do, and I think I've taken that to heart the most. I give 100 percent of my heart to everything I do and enjoy, and like you, I wear my emotions on my sleeve.

I love you so much and thank you for your service, as well as everything you have done for me. I am so proud to call you my papa and I love you.

Your grandson,
Jason

To my Papa,

It is hard to write down a lifetime of memories of a person who I consider to be the epitome of a grandfather. Sweet, loving, caring, hardworking and an allaround role model. It's unfortunate that I didn't grow up closer to Madison,  but it just made the time we have spent together that much sweeter.

Growing up, some of my fondest memories were driving up for Badger games and listening to your cassette tapes of the songs you wrote about Ron Dayne and the football program. When I played football in high school, I followed your footsteps playing Tight/Defensive End and wore your number 81 (even though the jersey was two sizes too small).

You came and spoke to my class in 5th grade about your experiences in the war. You took us fishing for Rainbow trout every year. Growing up, you made sure my room was filled with Badger posters autographed by players, coaches, and cheerleaders, but what you probably didn't realize is my favorite piece of memorabilia was the poster signed by you.

My grandpa is a walking legend in Madison. How cool is that? Papa, I said it'd be hard to write down a lifetime of memories and even though I haven't tackled them all in this letter, once I started writing, it was like a timeline of my most cherished times with you. Congratulations on this special day, on a lifetime of achievements and for continuing to make this grandson proud each and every day.

Love with all my heart,
Brian

Back Home Again in Madison

We arrived back home to Madison late at night and saw hundreds of people in the airport cheering our return. From the top of the escalator, we could hear the band and see that the airport was packed with people! It was an amazing sight! When we got down to the bottom of the escalator, I was greeted by two soldiers in dress uniform. They escorted me through the large crowds, which included: my wife Marion, her daughter Tara, our longtime friends including Lori Bilkey Sanders, her daughter Tori, Sue Anderson and her husband Gary, Bucky Badger,

and even the local TV news crew were there cheering for me. It was a day that I didn't want it to end. I can't even remember how many hands I shook or how many people I hugged that day. It was a very emotional homecoming and a day I will never forget.

15 Touchdowns

Marion and I were thrilled to receive one
of the Centennial plates ~ 2017

Centennial Celebration

In 2017, I turned 93 and Camp Randall Stadium turned 100!
There was a big tailgate and birthday party for me behind the
stadium. I was proud to be on the field with my grandson Brian,
and to be a part of the Centennial Celebration. It was really
something special to look up and see a close up of us on the
Jumbotron.

Honorable and proud moments with my grandson Brian ~ Camp Randall Stadium

An Unexpected Honor

On June 9, 2018, my friend Kevin Kirshbaum invited me to Dubuque, Iowa, to join him at the 55th Annual World Livestock Auctioneer Championship. My daughter and her friend Lori Bilkey Sanders joined me. What I didn't know when I accepted Kevin's invitation, was that I would be receiving an honorary award for my accomplishments and years as a livestock buyer.

Years ago, I was a livestock buyer in Beetown, which is in Grant County. That is where I first met Jimmy Kirschbaum,

Kevin's father. Jimmy had a farm with cattle there, and we used to meet at the sale barns. Jimmy and Kevin were hardworking men, and I taught them everything I knew about buying cattle. I helped them get started in business and they became very successful. Their success continues today at the *Livestock Exchange* in Bloomington, Wisconsin.

It was an unexpected honor that Jimmy and Kevin had arranged for me that day. I went into the sale barn to watch the auctioneer competition and everyone knew who I was and wanted to shake my hand. They all said I was clearly at home in that barn after spending 60 years in the business. Yes, it had been 60 years in "the business," but having been born and raised on a Wisconsin farm, it was in fact a lifetime. I was surprised and humbled to be recognized by these fine people in such a gratifying and humbling way.

An unexpected honor...with Cody Halverson and my dear friend Kevin Kirschbaum

Hall of Fame

Through the years, my alma mater, Dodgeville High School, has been very generous in recognizing alumni, including myself. In 2010, I was inducted into the Dodgeville High School's Hall of Fame. Following the football game there was a dinner and festivities. I was delighted to have Chuck Jr. and Renee join me as well as my grandson, Jason and Lori Bilkey Sanders.

Dear Students of Dodgeville High School

On May 16, 2018, I had the honor of again being recognized by Dodgeville High School. They unveiled my picture and it now hangs on the high school wall of distinguished alumni.

I was an honored to share my life story with the student body and faculty, alongside my daughter Renee ~ Dodgeville High School

There was a beautiful luncheon with all my friends and family in attendance. After lunch, they held a beautiful ceremony in my honor in front of the entire student body and all of the faculty. I was awarded a brick from the school and given a jersey. Then I gave a speech to the students and the staff. As I spoke, I looked out at all of the young faces of today's Dodgeville High School Dodgers and I thought about the many roads they would travel in their lives. It was unforgettable.

Gerry...One Year Later

It was an honor to be in the audience this past June as my friend Gerry Ayers was awarded as the Dodgeville High School distinguished alumni of the year. Gerry has been a longtime friend who has helped me through my years of fundraising for the Badgers. I am blessed to have Gerry and his family in my life.

Coach Bob Buck

Coach Bob Buck was also there to support the award recipients. He was a very successful head football and basketball coach at Dodgeville High School. Bob was inducted into the Wisconsin Basketball Hall of fame in 1995. He was also named to the *"Who's Who Among America's Teachers."* He is well respected in the community and a lifelong friend.

Standing with two of my great friends, Coach Bob Buck and Gerry Ayers ~ Dodgeville High School

16 Camp Randall Stadium

With Jason and Brian and my daughter Renee ~ Camp Randall Stadium

Lot 17

Every September, my daughter Renee and Lori, have planned birthday tailgates for me during a Badgers game. It has become a family tradition. Our friends Dave and Deanna Polley generously provide and grill the brats. The tailgates are held on the rooftop of Lot 17 on the north end of Camp Randall stadium. Renee and Lori usually arrive hours ahead to grab our favorite

Left upper corner: Ray Heim, Lori Bilkey Sanders, Bob Buck; Right upper corner: Rosie Koschkee, Marion Falch Halverson; Lower left corner: Dave Polley; Lower right corner: Deanna Balalock-Polley and me

spot near the elevator. On occasion, the UW band, directed by Michael Leckrone, has stopped by to play for us and to eat a few brats! Our space is decorated in Badger red and white. My jersey number 81 is hung high so people can find us. I hand out CDs of the songs that my brother Wayne and I wrote together, including the Ron Dayne song.

THE TALK
. by Doug Moe

'Dayne Song' poised for stardom

YOU MAY NOT be able got a program from the Iowa-UW football game, but you may soon be able to buy a cassette that includes an ode to Ron Dayne.

"The Great Dayne Song" was written by Madison castle buyer Chuck Halverson, with help from his brother Wayne Halverson, of Dodgeville. It is sung by longtime Common Faces vocalist Asa Mulra. Halverson said interest has been high from area radio stations and others, but he had been reluctant to try to market it on a tape cassette as long as Dayne was competing. He figured there had to be some NCAA rule against it; and he's probably right.

But with Dayne's eligibility about over, Halverson said he may market the song. "We'll add some others to it and see what happens."

Like many another enduring tune ("90 Bottles of

Beer on the Wall" comes to mind), "The Great Dayne Song" had its genesis on a bus ride. Halverson and some other Badger fans were going to an away game in Minnesota in Dayne's sophomore year when inspiration struck. Halverson played the entire song for me Friday, but I'll just share the chorus: "Come on Badger fans/If you want to have fun/Join us on the trail/Of the great, great one."

Given the current state of Dayneomania, he may have a hit on his hands. It would not be unprecedented. A punt return by halfback **Billy Cannon** that led LSU over Ole Miss 7-3 in 1959 when both schools were 6-0 inspired a song that for a long time got more radio play in the South than anything by Elvis. . . .

* * *

CANNON WON the Heisman Trophy that year, and Dayne appears a mortal lock for this year's award, which will be announced a week from today. On Wednesday I mentioned a New York Daily News story that said Yale's **Larry Kelley** was selling his

1936 trophy — the first-ever Heisman, according to the Daily News.

That's what I get for trusting a tabloid. Many readers took time to point out that the first Heisman was won by Jay Berwanger of Chicago in 1935. "Kelley was No. 2," **Bob Wahlers** wrote me. "I found this out while talking to **Bill Proxmire**, who was at Yale during that time." Wahlers concluded, "I didn't play football at Yale, but I did follow George Bush by several years as baseball captain." . . .

The critics were not overwhelmed by the movie adaptation of Wisconsin writer Jane Hamilton's novel "A Map of the World," which opened in limited release Friday. I mentioned this week that actress Sigourney Weaver spent some time at Hamilton's farm-apple orchard near Burlington to prepare for her role, which some think might win Weaver an Oscar. Mike Clark of USA Today wrote Friday, "Academy Award attention looks like a long-shot." . . . I heard from Stevens Point native Arthur Herman, today a history prof at Virginia's George

Mason University, whose new book "Joseph McCarthy: Re-examining the Life and Legacy of America's Most Hated Senator," was the catalyst for last Sunday's New York Times Magazine cover story. Herman did Jean Feraca's public radio show Thursday and told me Friday his book does not try to "rehabilitate" McCarthy. He said that "it's an attempt to understand why McCarthy had the hold he did in the '50s, and how his own personal flaws and hubris finally destroyed him." . . .

* * *

MOE KNOWS: The November issue of American Druggist magazine includes an upbeat look at State Street's Community Pharmacy, in a profile titled "A '70s-Style Pharmacy Enters the Millennium." It's "quite possibly America's only worker cooperative pharmacy," the magazine notes, and "has gained a reputation as a regional information source for alternative as well as prescription drugs." . . .

Heard something Moe should know? Please call 252-6446, e-mail him at dougmoe@madison.com or write to PO Box 8060, Madison, WI 53708.

Photo Courtesy of *Wisconsin State Journal*

FOLLOW THE TRAIL OF THE GREAT DAYNE

Come on Badger Fans, if you wanna to have fun.
Join us on the Trail of the GREAT, GREAT ONE.
He's known by the name of the GREAT DAYNE,
And he won't stop run-in "till he hits The Hall of Fame.

You gotta see him strut; you got to see him go,
Never in your life will you see such a show.
When his powers thru the line like a Greyhound Bus,
We'll all be so thankful he is a play'in for us.

He knocks those defensive backs-right on their hind,
Never stopping 'till he reaches the goal line.
He's the greatest running back you ever did see,
He's running in the Trail of the Heisman Trophy.

Now come on Badger Fans, if you wanna have fun,
Join us on the Trail of the GREAT, GREAT ONE.
He's known by the name of the GREAT DAYNE,
And some day he'll be sit-in' The Hall of Fame.

If any of our opponents never met the GREAT DAYNE,
They'll know him well-when they feel his pain.

(Chorus Repeat)
Come on Badger Fans,
if you wanna have fun,
Join us on the TRAIL of the
GREAT, GREAT ONE.
He's known by the name
of the GREAT DAYNE
And he won't stop a run-in' til
he hits THE HALL OF FAME.

Chuck & Wayne
Halverson
Copyright 1997

**Attending a Badger Fundraiser
with my wife Marion and
Ron Dayne**

Little Badgers

Last year, there was a new cheerleader added to the celebration, my great granddaughter, Adrianna! On June 28th, 2019 we welcomed my second great granddaughter, Camilla, and now we have another little Badger cheerleader in the making.

**Adrianna, cheering for
her Great Grandpa ~
Camp Randall Stadium**

17 The Story Continues

At home in my favorite place...
my Badger room

Running Country Roads

Some of the first memories of my childhood include running country roads. Little did I know that running the distance would be the foundation of who I would become. Whether I was racing to school, sprinting on the track or charging for a touchdown, I always tried to stay ahead of the game. My parents and siblings gave me the love and support I needed to become a high school graduate, a college football defensive end, a successful cattle-buyer, a proud parent, and now a Great Grandparent.

I consider myself to be a lucky and loved man as I look forward to my 95th birthday. I can't help but recall all of the extraordinary things I've seen that have come to pass, I remember the people who so profoundly touched my life and those who touched me and those who have passed on. Every Memorial Day I place a flower and say a prayer to all of my friends and family.

When I look back on all of the changes that have occurred since my days as a young boy on a farm in Jonesdale, I am amazed at all I have witnessed, from the events of WWII to the technology that allows me to communicate easily with my family. I am grateful for the progress but I also long for the simple days of walking bare-footed across the pastures to gather the cows for milking.

My wife, Marion, has been my dear companion for the past 15 years. She is devoted, caring and always patient. Our commitment to each other, our church and our children has strengthened our bond. I can't thank her enough for her continued love and support.

My son, Chuck Jr., is my "working memory." I can count on him to recall dates, events and to call me every day. Chuckie can bring a smile to my face and he lights up my life with his humor. I am so proud to call him my son.

I will be forever thankful to my daughter, Renee, for her long hours of listening, recording and orga-nizing the moments of my life. This book could not have been written without her help. Renee has been there many times throughout my life. Whether she was attending my golf outings, bringing the Honey Bears to cheer me on, or simply spending time with me. Renee has made my life complete.

As I offer my final words for family and friends, I would like to give some advice to live by: *Treat everyone the same, be honest and fair, don't be afraid to ask for help* and most importantly, *be the best at whatever you choose in life!* (I never wanted to be second!).

"I thank God for letting me live this long, and for my wonderful relationships with my family and friends."

~Chuck Halverson

Postscript
Renee Halverson Wright

I decided to write this book because my dad has lived a remarkable life, starting with his

humble beginnings as one of 17 children who grew up in a three-bed-room farm-house in rural Wisconsin to becoming one of the six WWII vets to be recognized for their service and participate in the 2015 Badger Honor Flight.

Through gathering notes and talking with my dad his stories gave me a clearer understanding of his life and all that he accomplished. More than any-thing, I cherish the hours we spent on the phone and I'm so grateful that my dad was able to come to Chicago for Father's Day to spend time with me and work on his book. Our numerous con-versations gave me a chance to see him as more than just my dad.

While my dad has documented so many mile-stones of his life, I would like to take a moment to share a few of mine. I remembered my dad spotted me when I did my first back-walkover for cheerleading tryouts, he prepared me to compete at the state track meet by driving his car as I ran behind him. My dad sewed the zipper in the high-heeled boots I wore to a school dance. More importantly, he gave me the guidance, support and unconditional love I needed to grow and succeed.

He taught me the difference between a Hail Mary pass versus an onside kick! He supported me in my dance career. My dad even bought season tickets to the Bears games, even though he was a Green-Bay Packers fan, just so he could watch me cheer. I remember a few times during the games, hearing my name shouted out from the fans in the south end zone, and I would smile knowing exactly who had started it...my precious dad, my very own cheerleader!

*In addition, I love that my dad taught me how to appreciate the little things in life like rooting for the Badgers, spending time with friends and creating family rituals that have lasted a lifetime. He gave me the opportunity to do whatever I wanted in life and the courage to go after my dreams. My dad is my Hero! Chuck Halverson is so much to so many but I am lucky and so proud to be able to call him my **Dad**!*

Happy 95th Birthday, Dad!

I love you to the moon and back!
Forever #81!

"From running country roads to walking with my grandsons...
my life has been blessed!"

Acknowledgments

Writing Consultants and Editing:
Lori Jill Klark & Laura Rincon-Camp

I would like to thank the following people for their help with remembering dates, rereading drafts, and giving permission to reproduce the photography for this book:

Renee Wright Halverson, my daughter
Chuck Jr. Halverson, my son
Marion, my wife
Alice Halverson, my dear sister
Connie Hendrickson
Dodge Point Country Club
Ed Obma Photography
Fred Anderson Cardinal Staff
Gary Davis
Joan Adcock, wife of Joe Adcock
Julie Wieskircher, daughter of Ellen Ann
Iowa County Historical Society
Lori Bilkey Sanders
Ludden Lake Country Club
Renee Carey Rizzo
The Dodgeville Chronicle,
Mike and Pat Reilly
Dodgeville High School
Wisconsin State Journal, Fred Anderson of the Cardinal Staff

The Jonesdale School Reunion Booklet
printed by Inkwell Printers Dodgeville, Wisconsin

Special Thanks:
To all the wonderful people who have shared their recollections,
photos, and precious time in the creation of this book.

Front Cover:
Concept, Renee Halverson Wright
Photo Courtesy of: *The Milwaukee State Journal*,
November 13, 1949

Back Cover:
Concept, Renee Halverson Wright

About the Author

RENEE HALVERSON WRIGHT is a former NFL cheer-leader. She is a professional dancer, choreographer, model, and actress. Her first book, *Missing from the Sidelines* was a four-year project. It required relentless determination to chronicle the extraordinary history of the Chicago Honey Bears.

Wright's new found passion for writing propelled her to collaborate with her father to write her second book, *Running Country Roads & Life Lessons Learned.* Telling her father's story was a true labor of love. Renee was born and raised in the small town of Dodgeville, Wisconsin, and currently resides in Chicago. While she loves the city life, she takes great pride in her roots as a small town girl.

Made in the USA
Middletown, DE
12 February 2020